AMERICA'S SHRINE
of DEMOCRACY
A Pictorial History

MOUNT RUSHMORE
HISTORY ASSOCIATION
Supporting Education at Mount Rushmore Since 1993

First Printing 1990

Second Printing 2004

Third Printing 2010

Published by the Mount Rushmore History Association

Written by T.D. Griffith

Art Direction & Design: Julie Sullivan Design, Flagstaff Arizona

Production: John Murdock Design

Project Manager & Editor: Debbie Ketel

Reviewed by Chief of Interpretation Jim Popovich (2004)

Printed in the U.S.A.

ISBN number: 978-0-9646798-6-3

Library of Congress Control Number: 2004101723

Mount Rushmore History Association; www.mtrushmorebookstore.com
13036 Hwy 244 . Keystone, SD 57751. 1-800-699-3142

As a committee of the Mount Rushmore National Memorial Society, the Mount Rushmore History
Association's mission is to support and assist the National Park Service with educational, historical,
and interpretive activities at Mount Rushmore National Memorial.

Dedicated to the nearly 400 drill-dusty miners

whose sweat, stamina, and stubborn determination

helped sculptor Gutzon Borglum mold an isolated mountain

in the middle of America into one of the

wonders of the modern world.

Photo courtesy of the Office of Ronald Reagan

In 1927, the American sculptor Gutzon Borglum began the mammoth task of turning the granite face of a mountain into the giant likenesses of four great Americans.

These four—Washington, Jefferson, Lincoln and Theodore Roosevelt—are the leaders whose ideals and principles would endure the test of time.

Even after the many years it will take to wear away these rock carvings, their ideals, the principles of democracy and freedom, will live on.

For more than 200 years now, this great country of ours has enjoyed the freedoms these four giants fought for.

So, let us cherish that freedom, and never lose sight of this Memorial and the men behind it.

Ronald Reagan

1990

Inset: National Park Service
Left: Rise Studio

AN UNLIKELY DREAM

It was an unlikely dream—a vision that would occupy the remaining years of one of America's most talented sculptors and result in the most colossal and compelling work of art in the world.

In December 1923, Doane Robinson, secretary and superintendent of the State Historical Society of South Dakota, began to act on a brainstorm. He approached an old acquaintance, the widely respected United States Senator Peter Norbeck, and proposed the unusual idea of hiring a monument sculptor to carve heroic figures somewhere in the Black Hills.

As the months passed, Norbeck was gradually won over by Robinson's reasonable contention that patriotic statuary on a scale larger than that of the Sphinx would draw national attention and tourism dollars to South Dakota.

Robinson envisioned famous Western figures, including Buffalo Bill Cody, Lewis and Clark, and notable Sioux Indians, carved from the granite spires of South Dakota's Needles.

Encouraged by Norbeck's response, Robinson introduced his plan in August 1924 to the famous sculptor Gutzon Borglum who was working amidst turmoil on another mountain carving project at Stone Mountain, Georgia.

Robinson's dream quickly captured Borglum's imagination, and the following month he made his first site-searching trip to the Black Hills. Borglum and his young son, Lincoln, were accompanied by Robinson, Dr. C.C. O'Harra, geologist-president of the South Dakota School of Mines at Rapid City, and mineralogist Dr. J.P. Connolly of that same institution.

After gazing at the impressive granite upthrusts of the Harney Range, Borglum would tell an admiring public that he had found "a veritable garden of the gods" in the Black Hills.

"I know of no grouping of rock formations that equals those found in the Black Hills," he said, "nor any that is so suitable to sculpture."

Doane Robinson, the "Father of Mount Rushmore."
South Dakota State Historical Society—State Archives

Charles E. Rushmore, New York City attorney.
National Park Service

Opposite Page: Mount Rushmore, a craggy granite upthrust, as Gutzon Borglum found it in the summer of 1925.
Rise Studio

Opposite Page Inset:
©Paul Horsted/dakotaphoto.com

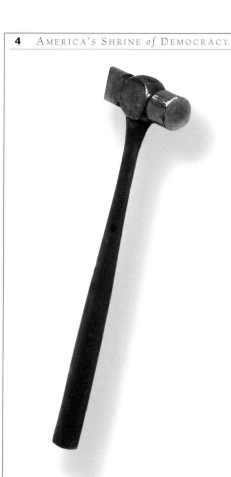

Right: Sculptor Gutzon Borglum and members of their search party stand on each other's shoulders to reach the 5,725-foot summit of Mount Rushmore.
Lincoln Borglum Collection

Opposite Page Inset: While camping in the Black Hills, young Lincoln Borglum listens as his father, seated at right, discusses the search for a "carveable" cliff with State Forester Theodore Shoemaker.
Lincoln Borglum Collection

Opposite Page Right: Gutzon Borglum unfurls the American flag on the crest of Mount Rushmore for the first time.
Lincoln Borglum Collection

By March 3, 1925, Norbeck and Congressman William Williamson had easily pushed through legislation permitting a massive mountain sculpture in the Harney National Forest. A corresponding bill in the state legislature faced considerably stiffer opposition, mainly on financial grounds, but by March 5, it too had passed.

During a visit to the Black Hills in August 1925, Borglum chose the actual site for the world's most monumental piece of sculpture — Mount Rushmore. The massive granite outcropping had not been named for an army general or an Indian fighter, but

more improbably, for a New York City attorney named Charles E. Rushmore who had visited the Black Hills several times on legal business in 1884 and 1885.

The sculptor knew right away that Mount Rushmore was ideal, because its southeast exposure provided the proper lighting and the granite mass was large enough to accommodate the planned sculpture.

With the aid of "horse, buffalo and dude wrangler" Ray Sanders, State Forester Theodore Shoemaker, and other Keystone residents, Borglum established a base camp at Mount Rushmore on August 17, 1925, and spent the next few days exploring the craggy granite cliff and sampling its rock. Borglum knew then that he had found his mountain.

While surveying the Black Hills one year earlier from the vantage of Harney Peak, the highest point between the Rockies and the Swiss Alps, Borglum had exclaimed, "Here is the place! American history shall march along that skyline."

The 57-year-old veteran artist could not have then known that organizing that march would present a struggle that would last the rest of his life — a struggle against seemingly insurmountable odds which would leave behind a monument that would stand for all time.

"Here is the place!

American

history shall march

along that skyline."

—*Gutzon Borglum*

It is often said that Gutzon Borglum knew what America wanted to say and the scale on which to say it.

Intensely patriotic, Borglum was a personal friend of four presidents and would often arrive unannounced at the White House, demanding to see the nation's chief executive. More often than not, his demands were met.

BORGLUM KNEW WHAT AMERICA WANTED TO SAY

By nature a romantic and dramatist, Borglum was his own salesman, as much as he was his country's. His flair for controversy and the media's willingness to quote much of what the brash young sculptor said led to many commissions, and undoubtedly to Mount Rushmore.

Born to Jens and Christina (Mikkelsen) Borglum in Ovid, Idaho, on March 25, 1867, Borglum was reared on the edge of America's frontier. The son of Danish immigrants, Borglum was as determined and proud as his parents, who had pushed and pulled their two-wheeled cart across 900 rugged miles of wilderness between the Missouri River and the "New Zion" that the Mormons were creating near Utah's Great Salt Lake.

At 16, Borglum ventured to California and became apprenticed to a lithographer. He began pursuing his love of art and soon found fulfillment in his painting. In 1888, he won a commission to paint the well-known explorer and mapmaker of the American West, General John Charles Fremont. The painting was a success, as was Borglum's new-found friendship with those who could help his career.

In particular, Borglum began taking lessons from Lisa Putnam, a widow 18 years his senior. In 1889, the two were married, and she began using her considerable social and professional contacts to advance her new husband's career.

One year later, Borglum and his bride set off for Europe, where he began studying sculpture under another new friend, the famous French sculptor Auguste Rodin. As the years progressed, Borglum began creating more and more sculpture, and as he became more well-known, he began receiving confidence-building commissions in the United States and Europe.

Above: An early attempt to embrace Mount Rushmore as the Eighth Wonder of the World uses the Great Sphinx to show the memorial's colossal size.
Lincoln Borglum Collection

**Above: Gutzon & Mary Borglum
spend a quiet moment with children
Lincoln and Mary Ellis.**
National Park Service

**Left: Borglum pauses during an
inspection of *The Aviator*. A model
of his *Seated Lincoln* is seen in the
background.**
Publisher's Photo Service

Above: Borglum poses before the projected image of his Confederate memorial at Stone Mountain, Georgia.
Brown and Dawson

But as Borglum's career flourished, his marriage foundered. In 1908, he and Lisa were divorced, and Borglum set sail for a return trip to the United States. On the ship, Borglum met the woman he would marry and never leave—Mary Montgomery.

Through a variety of commissions, the results of which expressed Borglum's unbridled vitality, energy, and emotion, the sculptor's reputation grew. In 1915, the Stone Mountain Confederate Memorial Association invited Borglum to Georgia with the hope of enticing the artist to render a memorial to the Confederate army.

The association had approached Borglum at the right time in his career. He agreed to undertake the massive work on a quarter-mile of mountain face, but World War I and the massive egos of all involved with the project would lead to its eventual destruction.

Shortly after the head of Confederate General Robert E. Lee was unveiled in 1924, a serious disagreement arose between the sculptor and the president of the Stone Mountain Association. On February 24, 1925, the association's board voted to dismiss Borglum from the work and hire another sculptor to finish the memorial according to Borglum's models and plans.

This, Borglum would not permit. After hopping a train to Atlanta, he immediately ordered the destruction of the working models and then hurried up the mountain and personally pushed the models of Lee's shoulders and Stonewall Jackson's head to the rocks below.

The ensuing verbal barrage from the association and others close to the project was intense. Borglum uncharacteristically sat out the brouhaha in North Carolina where his friend, Governor Angus McLean, refused to grant Georgia's request for extradition of the controversial sculptor.

Though he was often brash and egocentric, the Stone Mountain episode took its toll on Borglum. He told a friend he felt like a mother who had lost a child.

But when F. Scott Fitzgerald wrote, "There are no second acts in American lives," he did not have Gutzon Borglum in mind. And when Doane Robinson's letter inviting Borglum to South Dakota arrived, it could not have come at a more appropriate time. It offered Borglum vindication from the debacle at Stone Mountain. It offered Borglum a second act.

Above: Borglum's *Mares of Diomedes* was the first American-made sculpture purchased by The Metropolitan Museum of Art, New York City.
Publisher's Photo Service

Right: Borglum's *Pickett's Charge* was dedicated in 1929 at the Gettysburg Battlefield in Pennsylvania.
Publisher's Photo Service

Top Right: A unique photograph of Borglum and his beloved *Seated Lincoln*. The piece is now on display in Newark, NJ.
Lincoln Borglum Collection

"Beauty is like a soul that hovers over the surface of form. Its presence is unmistakable in Art or in Life. The measure of its revelation depends on the measure of our own soul-consciousness, the boundaries of our spirit."

Gutzon Borglum

VISIT BY
"SILENT CAL" SETS
THE STAGE

Supporters of Mount Rushmore were delighted in May 1927 when the White House announced that President Calvin Coolidge would spend his summer vacation in the Black Hills.

They quickly set about remodeling the State Game Lodge for use as the "Summer White House," stocking the newly renamed Grace Coolidge Creek with lunker trout and preparing for the presidential visit. Borglum made plans for a dedication of Mount Rushmore more fitting than the one conducted in 1925, despite Coolidge's assertion that he would make no formal appearances during his three-week stay.

Right: After being escorted to Mount Rushmore by Secret Service men on horseback, President Calvin Coolidge takes off his cowboy hat long enough to pledge federal funding to the project.
Lincoln Borglum Collection

But the pleasant climate of the Black Hills did wonders for the president's bronchitis, and he simply couldn't resist filling his creel with trout during his off-duty hours. The three-week sojourn quickly turned into a three-month vacation.

The extension allowed Senator Norbeck and Congressman Williamson enough time to persuade the president to dedicate this new monument known as Mount Rushmore.

The road to Mount Rushmore was not finished when Coolidge and his Secret Service escorts arrived at the memorial on horseback for formal dedication ceremonies on August 10, 1927. The president's entourage was greeted by more than 1,000 South Dakotans who hoped to catch a glimpse of him.

"We have come here to dedicate a cornerstone laid by the hand of the Almighty," Coolidge began. Then, in an eloquent speech that belied the verbal abilities of this Vermont farmboy, the president became the first to refer to Mount Rushmore as a "national shrine," and more importantly to Rushmore backers, he pledged federal support for the project.

Encouraged by the words of Calvin Coolidge, Borglum climbed the mountain and symbolically used six drill bits to begin the carving of the giant bust of George Washington. A short time later, he would begin refining the working models for Washington and his three compatriots—Thomas Jefferson, Abraham Lincoln, and Theodore Roosevelt.

Left: President Coolidge displays his ten-gallon hat while Senator Peter Norbeck, at his left, listens to other dignitaries during formal dedication ceremonies on August 10, 1927.
Lincoln Borglum Collection

Below: Lincoln Borglum measures the Jefferson figure while standing on his father's working model of the sculpture in this early hand-tinted plate.
Lincoln Borglum Collection

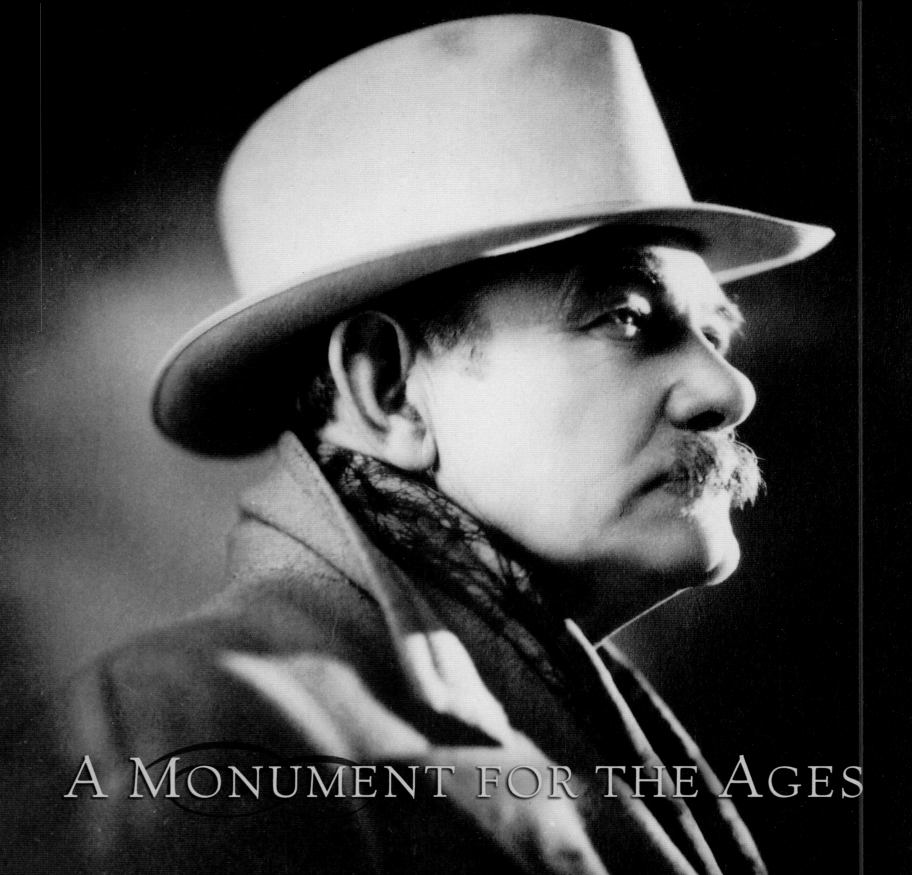

A MONUMENT FOR THE AGES

"We are not here trying to carve an epic, portray a moonlight scene, or write a sonnet; neither are we dealing with mystery or tragedy, but rather the constructive and dramatic moments or crises in our amazing history.

"We are cool-headedly, clear-mindedly setting down a few crucial, epochal facts regarding the accomplishments of the Old World radicals who shook the shackles of oppression from their light feet and fled despotism to people a continent; who built an empire and rewrote the philosophy of freedom and compelled the world to accept its wiser, happier form of government.

"Therefore, we believe a nation's memorial should, like Washington, Jefferson, Lincoln and Roosevelt, have a serenity, a nobility, a power that reflects the gods who inspired them and suggests the gods they have become.

"Hence, let us place there, carved high, as close to heaven as we can, the words of our leaders, their faces, to show posterity what manner of men they were. Then breathe a prayer that these records will endure until the wind and the rain alone shall wear them away."

THE FATHER *of our* COUNTRY

Above: Portrait of George Washington.
White House Historical Association

Opposite Page:
Bell Photo

Page 12: Sculptor John Gutzon de la Mothe Borglum, formal portrait, 1934.
Charles d'Emery

G utzon Borglum quickly dismissed Doane Robinson's suggestion that great Western characters provide the subject of the nation's newest mountain carving.

The sculptor opted instead for a memorial dedicated to the birth, growth, preservation, and development of a nation founded on the principles of democracy. Symbolized through the carved busts of George Washington, Thomas Jefferson, Abraham Lincoln, and Theodore Roosevelt, Mount Rushmore would be created as a monument not only to the four men depicted, but also to the ideals and aspirations of a nation they did so much to mold.

Borglum chose Washington for all the obvious reasons. As father of our country, Washington helped a nation shed the shackles of tyranny and build a new government with individual liberty as its cornerstone.

Born in 1732 to a wealthy Virginia family, Washington showed an early aptitude for surveying, and as a young man, mapped what was then the western wilderness. He first attracted attention in 1753 with a report of the French threat in the Ohio Valley and became commander in chief of the Virginia militia two years later.

In a wide-ranging career that included service as a member of the Virginia House of Burgesses, justice of the peace, commander in chief of the Continental Army, and finally, the nation's first chief executive, Washington would gain a reputation as a fearless leader of unparalleled integrity.

Thomas Jefferson would later write of Washington, "He was incapable of fear, meeting personal danger with the calmest unconcern … His integrity was the most pure, his justice the most inflexible, I have ever known; no motives of interest or consanguinity, of friendship, or hatred, being able to bias his decision. He was indeed, in every sense of the words, a wise, a good, and a great man …"

This is the manner in which Borglum tried to capture Washington on Mount Rushmore, and his reason for placing the first president as the dominant figure in the group.

Borglum modeled his Washington after the life mask created by French artist Jean Antoine Houdon during a visit to Mount Vernon in 1785, as well as portraits by Rembrant Peale and Gilbert Stewart.

After an exhaustive study of Washington's character and appearance, Borglum once told a friend, "I'll show you a Washington at Valley Forge who had the courage to freeze his dreams into reality that bitter winter when he faced every form of defeat and discouragement."

Liberty

"The preservation of the sacred fire of liberty, and the destiny of the Republican model of government are justly considered as deeply, perhaps as finally staked, on the experiment entrusted to the hands of the American people."

George Washington,
First Inaugural Address,
April 30, 1789

A WESTWARD VISION

Above: Portrait of Thomas Jefferson.
White House Historical Association

Opposite Page:
Bell Photo

Although Borglum selected George Washington and Abraham Lincoln as subjects for Mount Rushmore early in the planning stages of the project, there was little opposition when he announced that Thomas Jefferson would join the group.

Jefferson, born the son of a Virginia planter in 1743, had served as governor of his native state, drafted the Declaration of Independence at age 33, was minister to France, spent four years as secretary of state under Washington, and finally served two terms as the nation's third president. Those contributions alone should have provided the rationale for his inclusion on Mount Rushmore.

But Borglum believed Jefferson's contributions as president had greater impact. Specifically, the sculptor admired Jefferson's vision of a nation that stretched from coast to coast, and even more so, the president's ability to negotiate what is widely regarded as the best real estate bargain of all time.

When French General Napoleon Bonaparte persuaded the Spanish to return the province of Louisiana to France in 1800, President Jefferson received the reports with alarm. He immediately sent his envoys to Napoleon in hopes of buying New Orleans and other strategic parts of Louisiana from France. Much to their surprise, Napoleon, who was expecting a renewed war with England, agreed to sell the vast Louisiana Territory to the U.S. in April 1803, and the envoys quickly agreed to the total purchase price of $15 million.

Although the purchase had greatly exceeded Jefferson's instructions, colonial Americans viewed the purchase of 828,000 square miles at about three cents an acre as a triumph that more than doubled the land mass of the young republic. Even with the purchase, Jefferson balanced the budget, reduced the national debt, and was re-elected in 1804.

Despite his intense interest in the nation's western development, Borglum elected to portray Jefferson at age 33, his age when he drafted the Declaration of Independence. Using the life mask of Jefferson created by American artist John H.I. Browere as his model, Borglum attempted to render the president on Mount Rushmore as a young man, full of the dreams, hope, and fervor that had led to one of the nation's most treasured documents.

The Jefferson figure originally was started at Washington's right. After about 18 months of work on the bust, crews ran into faulty rock and were forced to blast the figure from the face of the mountain. Borglum then had his crew begin work on Jefferson to Washington's left. Despite encountering fissures and crags at the new location, workers were able to complete the Jefferson figure there, and that is where the nation's third president will rest for centuries, staring heavenward.

Equality

"We hold these truths to be

self-evident, that all men are

created equal, that they are

endowed by their creator with

certain unalienable rights,

among these are life, liberty,

and the pursuit of happiness."

Thomas Jefferson,
Declaration of Independence,
July 4, 1776

The GREAT EMANCIPATOR

Above: Portrait of Abraham Lincoln.
White House Historical Association

Opposite Page:
Bell Photo

Turn-of-the-century artists were known for their sculptures of the beloved Abraham Lincoln, and Gutzon Borglum was no exception.

Overtly fond of the nation's 16th president, Borglum would sketch him on restaurant napkins and mentioned him in the same breath as Washington in his first proposal for Mount Rushmore.

Born in a log cabin in the backwoods of Kentucky and raised in poverty, Lincoln's parents were barely literate. In 1831, he set up house in New Salem, Illinois, and taught himself law, eventually becoming one of the most respected lawyers in the state. He served seven years in the Illinois Legislature and retained his rough, frontier manners even after a well-connected marriage to Mary Todd in 1842.

Five years later, Lincoln gained a seat in the U.S. House of Representatives, but his opposition to the Mexican War lost him many supporters and eventually his House seat. In 1858, he contested the seat of Senator Stephen Douglas and challenged him to a series of historic debates that, even though he lost the election, established Lincoln as an orator of national stature. In 1860, he was nominated as a presidential candidate by the Republican party, winning against a split Democratic vote.

Before he took office, seven Southern states already had seceded from the Union. Determined to hold the nation together, Lincoln built up the army, blockaded Southern ports, and personally directed strategy as commander in chief until he gave Ulysses S. Grant command of the armies in the field in March 1864. Despite early setbacks for the North, Lincoln's patience, fortitude, and fierce devotion to the nation helped preserve the Union, which he saw as a bastion of democratic government.

On April 9, 1865, Confederate General Robert E. Lee surrendered. Five days later, Lincoln was shot at the Ford Theatre by John Wilkes Booth and died early on the morning of April 15.

Borglum had gained widespread acceptance for his portrayals of Lincoln prior to coming to the Black Hills. His marble portrait of the *Great Emancipator* on permanent display in the rotunda of the U.S. Capitol and the *Seated Lincoln* are among the most magnificent Lincolns ever created.

After studying Clark Mill's life mask of Lincoln from every angle and a half-dozen photographs Borglum believed to be accurate, the sculptor elected to portray Lincoln with the beard he wore during his presidency. Borglum, who admired Lincoln more than any other American, would capture the great president's compassion in heroic dimensions while establishing himself as the premiere sculptor of his day.

In 1938, Borglum responded to a question about the selection of Abraham Lincoln for Mount Rushmore by writing, "Lincoln, because it was Lincoln and no other than Lincoln, whose mind, heart, and finally life, determined that we should continue as a common family of states and in union forever."

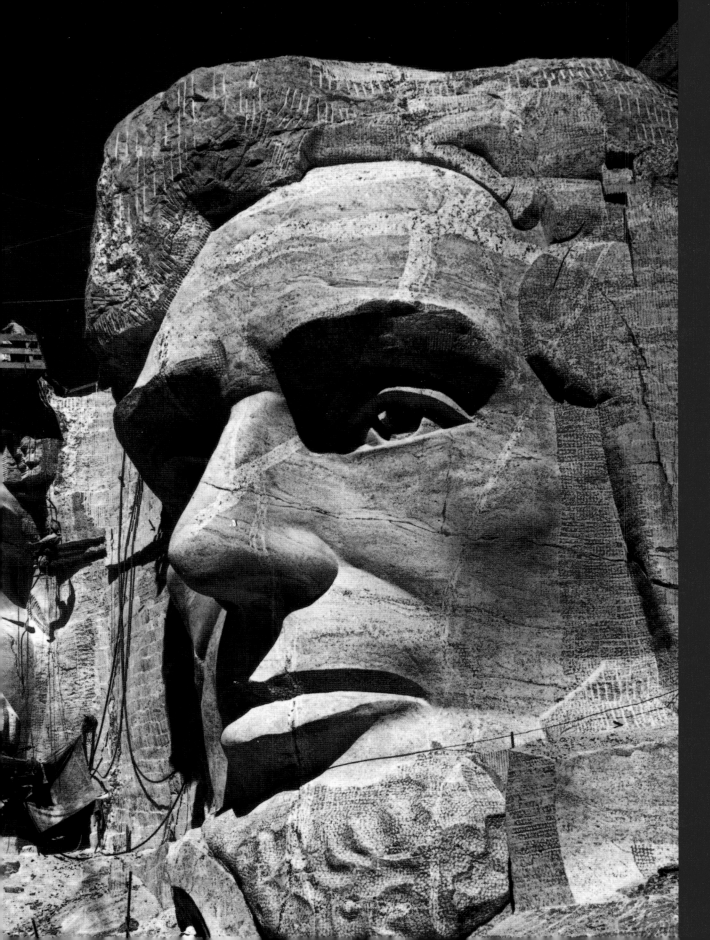

Unity

"It is rather for us to be here dedicated to the great task remaining before us—that from these honored dead we take increased devotion to that cause for which they gave the last full measure of devotion…that this nation, under God, shall have a new birth of freedom—and that government of the people, by the people, for the people, shall not perish from the earth."

Abraham Lincoln,
Gettysburg Address,
November 19, 1863

The EPITOME *of* AMERICA'S SPIRIT

Above: Portrait of Theodore Roosevelt.
White House Historical Association

Opposite Page:
Bell Photo

The selection of Theodore Roosevelt for Mount Rushmore's fourth subject drew a great deal of criticism. Many believed that history had not had time enough to judge the nation's 26th president. But, Gutzon Borglum saw Roosevelt as the epitome of the American spirit and individuality that had made a young nation great.

Borglum simply identified with "TR's" energy, charisma, and willingness to lead the most robust life imaginable. The two had been close friends, and Borglum had gladly campaigned for Roosevelt during the statesman's unsuccessful 1912 bid aboard the Bull Moose rebellion.

Born in 1858 to the prosperous New York Roosevelt clan, Theodore was sickly in his youth, yet driven to overcome adversity in whatever form it presented itself. He was at different times a progressive and conservative. His great energy often took him outside of politics on numerous hunting and exploring expeditions.

Roosevelt published more than 2,000 works on history, biology, politics, and his travels. A graduate of Harvard, he married Alice Hathaway Lee in 1880. Four years later, his wife and his mother would die on the same day, leaving Roosevelt with a broken heart and a motherless daughter. He sought solace in the bleak badlands of the Dakota Territory, where he became a rancher near present-day Medora, North Dakota.

Returning to New York, Roosevelt remarried and unsuccessfully sought election as New York City mayor. He later established a reputation as an efficient administrator while serving as commissioner for the Civil Service and the New York City police. As assistant secretary of the Navy in 1897-98, Roosevelt advocated the buildup of a strong fleet.

When war broke out with Spain, he joined it in Cuba with his famous volunteer cavalry troop, the Rough Riders. Most of the troop consisted of the unpolished friends he made during his stint in the Dakota Territory. Roosevelt returned from the Battle of San Juan Hill a national hero and for two years served as governor of New York. He was persuaded to run as vice president with William McKinley in 1900 and took over the presidency on September 14, 1901 when McKinley died from an assassin's bullet.

A Roosevelt biographer once wrote that it was the only time in America's history when the most interesting man in America was the president of the United States. At 42, he was the youngest president in history, the first president to travel out of the country while in office, the first to win the Nobel Peace Prize, and the first to have a black man dine at the White House.

He was America's "trust buster," a friend of the common man. And, Roosevelt was the nation's first conservation president, creating five new national parks, 15 national monuments, the first federal game preserve, 16 federal bird refuges, and 13 new national forests.

But those high achievements were not what led Borglum to cast Roosevelt's face on the side of a cliff for all eternity. "Roosevelt is joined with the others because he completed the dream of Columbus, opened the way to the East, joined the waters of the great East and West seas," Borglum wrote, in reference to the Panama Canal begun during Teddy's tenure as president of the United States.

Bravery

"We, here in America, hold in

our hands the hopes of the

world, the fate of the coming

years; and shame and disgrace

will be ours if in our eyes the

light of high resolve is dimmed,

if we trail in the dust the golden

hopes of men."

Theodore Roosevelt,
Address at Carnegie Hall,
March 30,1912

BEHIND THE SCENES: MOTIVATED MEN

MOUNT RUSHMORE
NATIONAL MEMORIAL SOCIETY
Contributing To Mount Rushmore's Success Since 1930

Above: Today, the Society continues to play an active role in the development and preservation of the memorial in cooperation with the National Park Service.

Opposite Page Left: The original Mount Rushmore National Memorial Commission poses in front of the mountain on July 17, 1929.
Back row (l-r): Delos B. Gurney, Joseph S. Cullinan, Charles M. Day
Front row (l-r): John A. Boland, Julius Rosenwald, Doane Robinson, Gutzon Borglum, William Williamson, Frank O. Lowden, Fred Sargent, Royal C. Johnson, Mrs. Lorine Jones Spoonts.
Bell Photo

Although the nation's Shrine of Democracy is rightfully attributed to Gutzon Borglum's creative genius, it is also true that Mount Rushmore never would have been completed without the assistance of some other instrumental Americans.

Soon after the formal dedication by Calvin Coolidge, the 60-year-old Borglum came to the realization that he now had to carry through with his grand vision and create a mountain carving using techniques that had yet to be invented. Compounding the great sculptor's problems were his own financial woes which, despite his well-known artistic talents and numerous commissions, would plague him until his death in a Chicago hospital on March 6, 1941.

Fortunately, supporters of this new venture called Mount Rushmore were well aware of his lack of business acumen and took the necessary steps to ensure that funds donated to the project were used wisely.

Senator Peter Norbeck, twice governor of South Dakota and a personal friend of President Coolidge, lent his powerful Washington influence to the project at an early stage. The stocky, 225-pound "benevolent buffalo" would carry on Doane Robinson's dream when the state historian no longer had the political clout to secure federal funding for the project.

Norbeck also enlisted the aid and sound legislative ability of William Williamson, a tall, unpretentious representative from South Dakota's third congressional district. Together, the two sons of Norwegian immigrant homesteaders would help ensure Mount Rushmore's place in American history.

John Boland Sr., a farm implement dealer with an abundance of business sense, was also a steadfast booster of the planned mountain carving while serving as mayor of Rapid City. His sound advice and frugal manner frustrated the spendy Borglum, and there were often fiery clashes between the two. But like the others who scraped up dollars for Rushmore during the lean years of the Great Depression, Boland would fall in love with this novel idea, lend his own money to Borglum, and find his rightful place in the history books.

In addition to a cast of colorful characters who helped Borglum realize his dream, three organizations would eventually assume the financial and moral responsibility of seeing Mount Rushmore through to its completion.

The Mount Harney Memorial Association, established by the state legislature in 1925, was first authorized to "carve a memorial in heroic figures" in the Black Hills. The association entered into a formal contract with Borglum when work commenced on the mountain in 1927.

When federal funds were appropriated in 1929, the Mount Rushmore National Memorial Commission was established. The commission assumed financial responsibility for the project in its early stages.

The necessity to solicit private funds to match federal appropriations and to provide citizen involvement in the memorial prompted formation of the Mount Rushmore National Memorial Society in Washington, D.C. on February 24, 1930. Through sale of memberships, operation of concessions, and generating publicity for the mammoth mountain carving, the Society amassed funds that, when matched with federal monies, contributed greatly to early progress on the sculpture.

Today, the Society continues to play an active role in the development and preservation of the memorial in cooperation with the National Park Service.

Top to Bottom:
Rapid City Businessman John Boland, Sr.
Boland Family

Senator Peter Norbeck.
South Dakota State Historical Society

Congressman William Williamson.
National Park Service

THE CENTER OF A CONTINENT

When Gutzon and Lincoln Borglum arrived in the Black
Hills in the summer of 1925, they found an emerald island in a vast sea of
prairie, a place of lofty ponderosa pines, rushing streams, and towering granite peaks.

"This Black Hills country has charm...a lingering kind of human satisfaction for the
soul...Round about you, rugged strengths, forest depths, primeval earth at best..."
architect Frank Lloyd Wright wrote after visiting his friend Borglum at the sculptor's ranch.

Until Borglum arrived and brought a flurry of presidential
visits and nationwide publicity spanning several decades,
the Black Hills was content to be a family vacation spot with
regional appeal.

But visits by Calvin Coolidge in 1927 and Franklin D.
Roosevelt in 1936, combined with steady progress on the
mountain memorial and the Black Hills, began to attract publicity.
Not since 10,000 gold seekers followed General George Custer's
7th Cavalry into the Hills 50 years earlier had western South Dakota experienced such
attention. And if not for the brash Borglum and the greatest monument on earth,
residents might have been a little overwhelmed by the public glare.

But when family travelers finally found the Black Hills, they became enchanted
with its setting, its wildlife, and its underground wilderness. They found buffalo and
antelope grazing on open prairies and deer and elk roaming the mountain meadows.
Jagged peaks, cool streams, and a subterranean labyrinth of limestone caverns were
meant for exploring.

As four faces of freedom formed on a mountain in the sacred land of the Lakota, so
too evolved an elaborate hospitality industry to serve the needs of the visitor. New hotels,
motels, campgrounds, resorts, and attractions sprang to life with the presidents, and the
region began to enjoy a new economic prosperity independent of agriculture.

Left: Badlands National Park.
Johnny Sundby Photography

**Inset: Pasque Flower, South Dakota's
state flower.**
South Dakota Tourism

"This Black Hills country

has charm...a lingering

kind of human satisfaction

for the soul...Round about

you, rugged strengths,

forest depths, primeval

earth at best..."

Frank Lloyd Wright,
Architect

Above: A bison bull saunters through the forest in Custer State Park. Bison can weigh a ton and outrun a horse.
South Dakota Tourism

Left: Mounted riders take part in the annual Custer State Park Buffalo Round-Up, one of the most exciting spectator events in the Black Hills.
South Dakota Tourism

Opposite Page: Rocky Mountain goats are frequent visitors to the four famous faces at Mount Rushmore.
©Paul Horsted/dakotaphoto.com

Above: As the world's third longest cave, Jewel Cave National Monument has nearly 130 miles of known passageway and is home to exceptionally rare formations.
South Dakota Tourism

Left: Granite cliffs and outstanding scenery make the Black Hills a popular destination for rock climbers.
South Dakota Tourism

Today, visitors to the Black Hills still find an emerald oasis, a place where granite peaks and dark pines blanket an area the size of Delaware. Within the Hills, they find a national forest, a national park, two national monuments, Mount Rushmore National Memorial, and the third largest state park in the nation.

The multi-hued moonscape of Badlands National Park, with 243,302 acres of ridges, gorges, and pinnacles shaped over a half-million years, flanks the Hills' eastern edge. Across the South Dakota border, in northeast Wyoming, Devils Tower juts 865 feet into the air as the country's first national monument, established by Theodore Roosevelt in 1906.

Highways designed and built for sight-seers thread through the granite spires of Custer State Park, which at 71,000 acres, is the third largest state park in the United States.

No less remarkable are the numerous caves found in a limestone racetrack that circles the Black Hills. Jewel Cave National Monument and Wind Cave National Park are the third and sixth longest in the world, respectively, and their unusual crystal formations and vast underground lakes have established them as world-class havens for cavers.

While Mount Rushmore continues to provide the focal point for visits to the Black Hills, residents and visitors have become infatuated with the lure of a land filled with rich history, abundant wildlife, and natural beauty—a veritable garden of the gods.

Above: The woodlands and wildflower-studded meadows of the Black Hills provide excellent opportunities for hikers and mountain bikers on the Mickelson Trail.
South Dakota Tourism

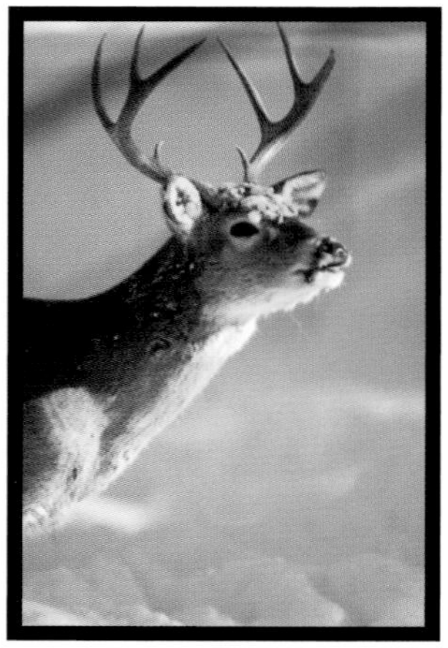

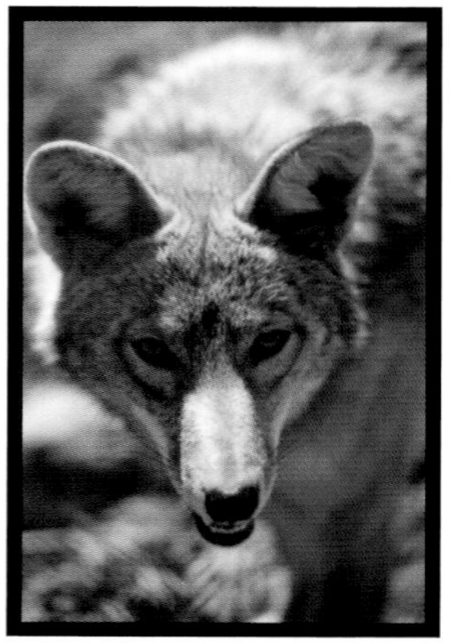

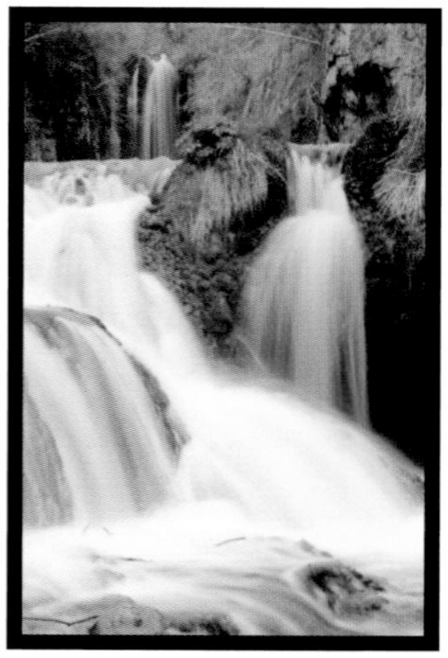

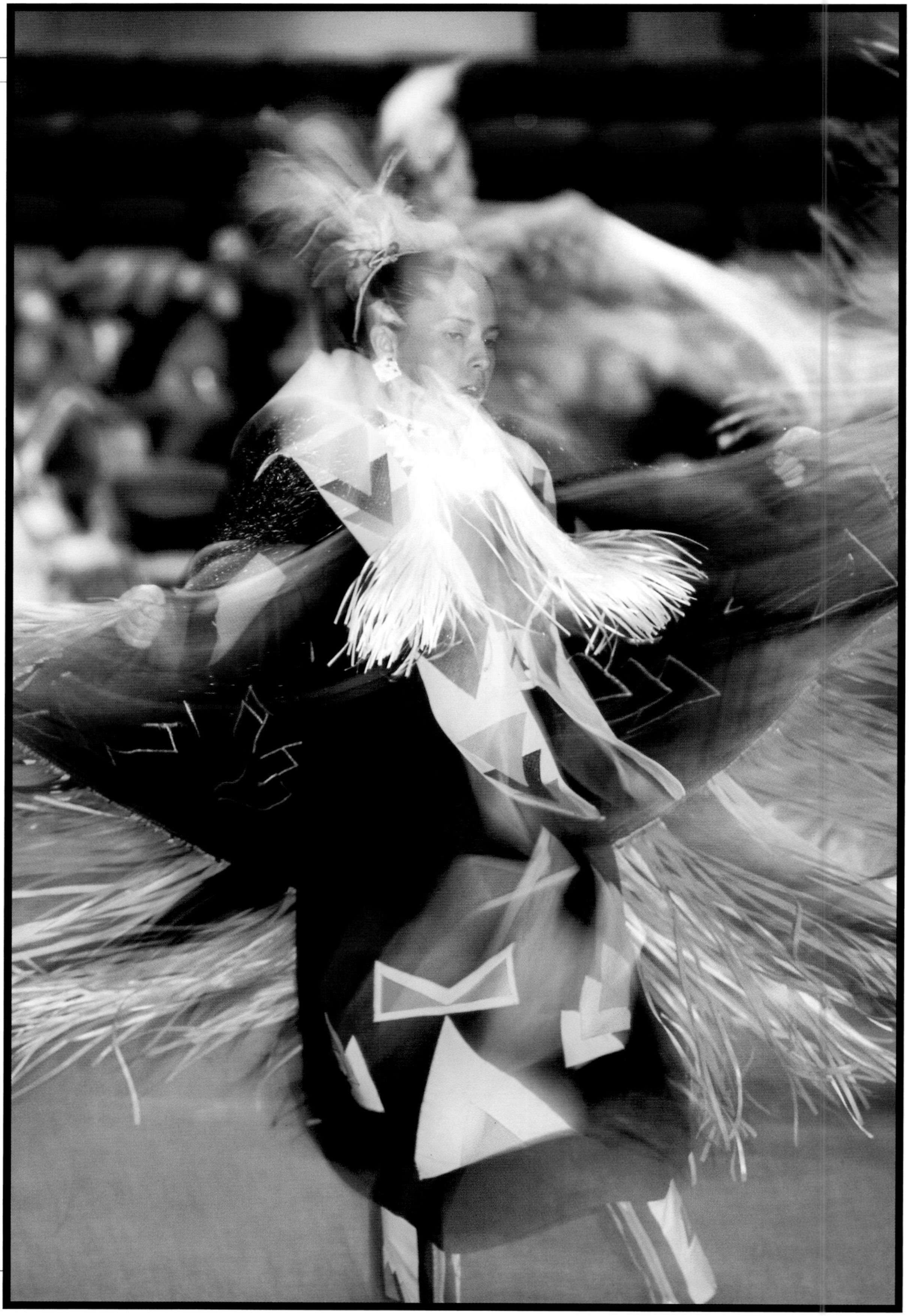

Above: Mount Rushmore is framed in one of several tunnels found on the twisting Iron Mountain Road.

Left: A view of The Needles from Little Devils Tower in Custer State Park.

Opposite Page Top to Bottom: A whitetail deer forages for food in a wintry Black Hills forest.

South Dakota's State Animal, the coyote, poses for a portrait.

Cascading alpine streams and outstanding trout fishing are found throughout the Black Hills.

Opposite Page: A Pow Wow dancer whirls in a maze of color in one of many tribal customs that celebrate Native American heritage.

Photos courtesy of South Dakota Tourism

AN ERA *of*
CONFIDENCE

As Mount Rushmore depicts the will of a free nation through the carved busts of four great presidents, so too it symbolizes a special era in the life of a young republic. Had the times been different, it is questionable whether this mammoth mountain memorial would have been attempted, let alone completed.

When President Coolidge traveled to the Black Hills in 1927, the post-war economy was strong. Inflation hovered at .5%, and unemployment stood at 3.3%. Wampole's cod liver oil was a buck, and a bar of Ivory Soap set shoppers back eight cents.

America said good-bye to notorious Lizzie Borden that year and hello to the juke box, car radios, and Movietone News. After becoming the first to fly solo across the Atlantic, Charles Lindbergh returned home in May 1927 to 3.5 million letters containing 7,000 job offers.

In Chicago, 104,943 turned out to watch Gene Tunney, down for "the long count," rise to defeat Jack Dempsey. Al Capone's gang netted $175 million in liquor, protection money, gambling, vice, and the rackets after his goons gunned down six of Bugs Malone's men in the St. Valentine's Day massacre.

Instilled with confidence and prosperity, America could afford to be generous and fund such extravagances as a mountain carving. In fact, "Silent Cal" Coolidge suggested as much when he took time out of his vacation to dedicate Mount Rushmore.

Above: Calvin Coolidge poses in full western regalia.
Smithsonian Archives

Right: An early Ivory Soap advertisement.
Advertising Museum Archives

IVORY SOAP
- kind to everything it touches -
99 44/100% PURE ▪ IT FLOATS

Above: Charles Lindbergh and the Spirit of St. Louis.
Smithsonian Archives

Left: Taking every opportunity to tell the world of his monumental dream, sculptor Gutzon Borglum speaks to the crowd at the dedication of the Washington figure July 4, 1930.
Rise Studio

Left Below: A Rushmore pin from 1931 with the presidents in the wrong order—Washington, Jefferson, Lincoln, Roosevelt.
Bonita Cochran Ley Collection

Despite the rhetoric, it was not until February 1929 that Coolidge made good on his pledge and, in one of his last official acts as president, signed a federal appropriation for Mount Rushmore. Because the federal monies were distributed on a matching basis, the small core of Rushmore's active supporters scrambled to secure private donations to keep construction moving. As the giant likeness of Washington emerged from the rock and crews began clearing a spot for Jefferson to Washington's right, the first full season of work at Rushmore came to an end.

By July 4, 1930, Borglum felt the Washington portrait was ready for unveiling. So, on that clear, crisp summer day, with a 21-gun salute, a crowd of well-wishers, and a giant flag stitched by local women, the sculpted bust of the nation's first president was officially dedicated.

THE ART OF CARVING A MOUNTAIN

The amount of rock to be removed made dynamite a practical necessity. Rushmore's powdermen, under the watchful eye of Borglum, became so skilled in removing the precise amounts of rock that they could block out a nose to within an inch of the finished surface, shape the lips, and grade the contours of the neck, cheeks, and brows.

During the final years of construction, Lincoln Borglum was entrusted with "pointing," the method of transferring measurements from the sculptor's model to the mountain. Using booms, plumb bobs, a complex measuring system, and a mountain, Borglum and his crews would duplicate the 1/12th-scale model that is still found today in the Sculptor's Studio at Mount Rushmore.

As work neared the finished surface, greater caution was exercised to avoid damaging the rock. Workers suspended in bosun chairs and others on scaffolding drilled a series of holes in the mountain in a process known as "honeycombing." Then, they took hammers and wedges to remove the excess rock. In the final stage, a "four-star" bit was placed in the pneumatic drill for the "bumping" process, which left the surface as smooth as a concrete sidewalk.

Although often stalled by inadequate funding and inclement weather, visits by Presidents Calvin Coolidge and Franklin Roosevelt, movie stars, media, and moguls kept Mount Rushmore in the news and on America's mind. All told, the memorial would cost $989,993.32 to complete. Private contributions, including donations from business, industry, and individuals, as well as nickels, dimes, and pennies from school children, aided early progress on the carving. But, in the end, federal appropriations accounted for $836,000.

Following Gutzon's death and a petition signed by Rushmore workers, the Mount Rushmore Memorial Commission appointed Lincoln to carry on the work. With funds dwindling and the European situation growing more critical, Lincoln and a skeleton crew spent the final seven months refining the work to its present state.

On October 31, 1941, Lincoln and his remaining men stowed their tools, packed up their belongings, and left the mountain, returning it to the eternal silence from which they had awakened it 14 years earlier.

Above: Borglum with his models in the Sculptor's Studio.
Lincoln Borglum Collection

Left: A dusting of snow cloaks the presidents in white.
National Park Service

SCHRAMM

ROCK DRILLS
PAVING BREAKERS
TAMPERS, SPADES &
ACCESSORIES

SCHRAMM INC.   AIR COMPRESSORS   WEST CHESTER, PA.
BULLETIN · PRICE LIST NO. CW-17

Left: Perched in the hoist house on top of Washington's head, Alfred Berg and Jack "Palooka" Payne were responsible for six winches used to raise and lower drillers sitting in their bosun chairs.
Bell Photo

Below Left: Only the fireplaces of the original Sculptor's Studio remain today. Borglum and his working models moved to the present studio in 1939.
Publisher's Photo Service

Opposite Page: Gutzon Borglum, wearing his customary scarf no matter the season, directs drillers in work on the granite faces.
Bell Photo

Below: A powderman, John Johnson, prepares charges for the afternoon blast on the monument.
Rise Studio

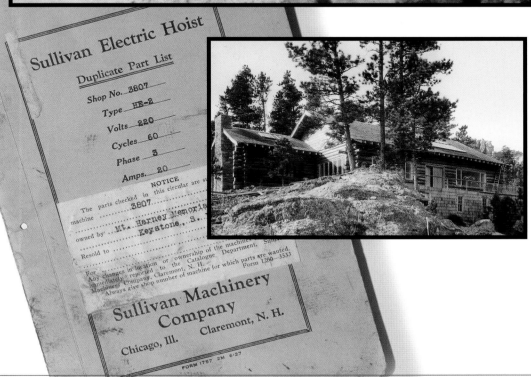

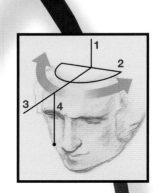

BORGLUM'S POINTING SYSTEM
The differences between the models in the Sculptor's Studio and the heads on the mountain show how Borglum fine-tuned the four granite giants into true works of art.

The models were sized at a ratio of 1:12— one inch on the model would equal one foot on the mountain. A metal shaft (1) was placed upright at the center of the model's head. Attached at the base of the shaft was a protractor plate (2), marked in degrees, and a horizontal ruled bar (3) that pivoted to measure the angle from the central axis. A weighted plumb line (4) hung from the bar. It slid back and forth to measure the distance from the central head point and raised and lowered to measure vertical distance from the top of the head. Thus, each point on the model received three separate measurements. The numbers were then multiplied by 12 (angles remained the same) and transferred to the granite face via a large-scale pointing mechanism anchored at the top of the mountain.

NPS Illustration/Susan Barkus
Text compliments of Harper's Ferry

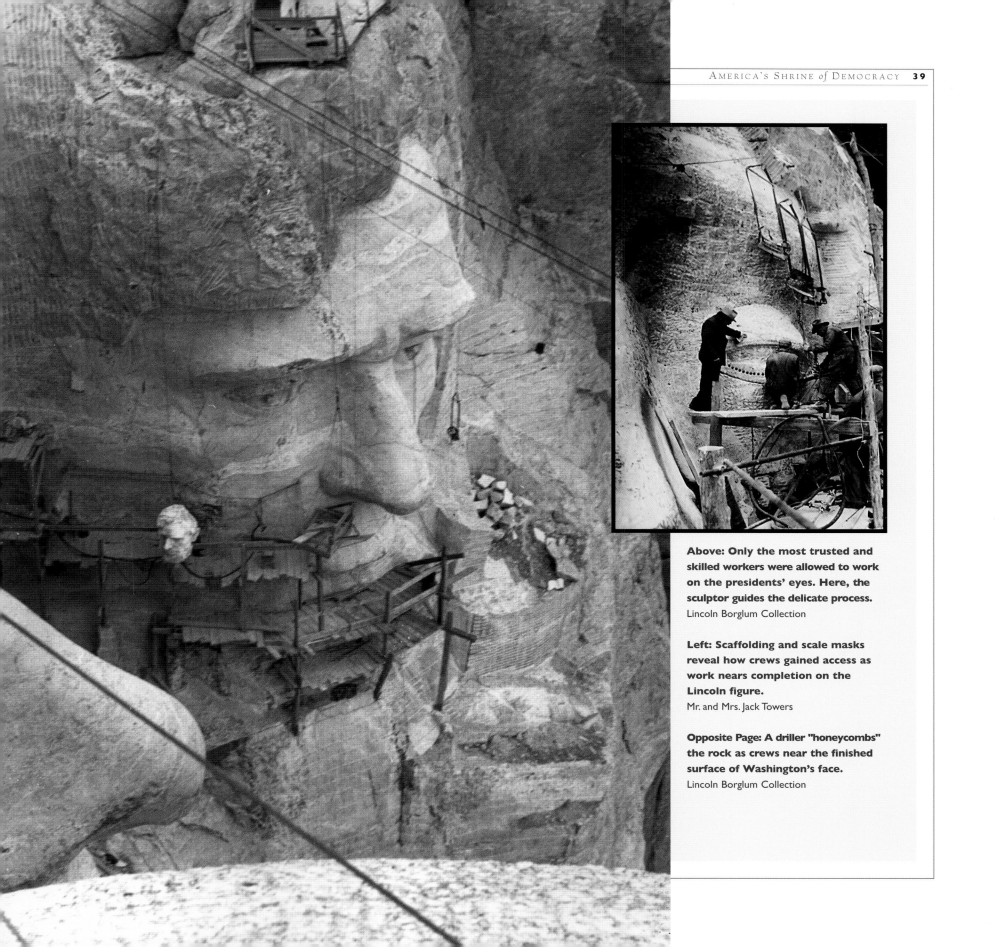

Above: Only the most trusted and skilled workers were allowed to work on the presidents' eyes. Here, the sculptor guides the delicate process.
Lincoln Borglum Collection

Left: Scaffolding and scale masks reveal how crews gained access as work nears completion on the Lincoln figure.
Mr. and Mrs. Jack Towers

Opposite Page: A driller "honeycombs" the rock as crews near the finished surface of Washington's face.
Lincoln Borglum Collection

"Don't say 'I can't' on this work
The 'I can'ts' are unknown
in the world's work and
unremembered in history."

Gutzon Borglum

Left: Mount Rushmore in 1939. The road seen in the photograph was later realigned and replanted with ponderosa pines, eventually becoming the bed for the Presidential Trail.
Lincoln Borglum Collection

Opposite Page: Still surrounded by swing seats and scaffolding, the four presidents have emerged from the rock in the summer of 1941. Gutzon Borglum died in March 1941, and his son, Lincoln, carried on the finishing work.
Rise Studio

FRANKLIN ROOSEVELT ADDS PRESTIGE

Right: Borglum explains his grand vision to President Roosevelt and then South Dakota Governor Tom Berry during the dedication ceremonies.
Black Hills Studio

Below Right: Borglum presents FDR with a medallion during a private moment in the president's 1936 visit to Mount Rushmore. Following the 1936 dedication of Jefferson, Lincoln was dedicated on September 17, 1937, and Roosevelt was unveiled on July 2, 1939.
International News Photos, Inc.

Opposite Page: Although not scheduled to speak at the Jefferson dedication in 1936, Franklin Roosevelt was so moved by what he saw that he grabbed network microphones, as his son, Franklin Jr., assisted.
Bell Photo

SOUVENIR PHOTOGRAPHS OF

Rushmore Memorial

BLACK HILLS, SO. DAK.

Donated by Mr. & Mrs. Jerrel and Patricia Busey

"I had seen the photographs

and the drawings of this

great work. And yet, until

about ten minutes ago,

I had no conception of its

magnitude, its permanent

beauty and its importance."

Franklin D. Roosevelt
Jefferson Dedication
August 30, 1936

HALL *of* RECORDS:
COMPLETING
A DREAM

Gutzon Borglum's dream of Mount Rushmore did not end at the sculpted faces of four great presidents. His vision included an 800-step Grand Stairway leading to the Hall of Records in a deep canyon directly behind the carving.

From the ageless granite of that hidden canyon, Borglum planned to carve another slice of history — an impregnable repository for the nation's most treasured artifacts, including the Constitution and the Bill of Rights, the busts of outstanding Americans, and documents explaining how and why Rushmore was carved.

"Into this great hall, beautiful as a temple, we will place records, the new records, the purely American records, of released souls, of great inventors..." Borglum wrote.

His greatest fear was that future civilizations would have no idea why these four giants adorned a mountain in the middle of America.

Armed with that mission, Borglum put a crew to work on the Hall in July 1938. A year later, drillers had cut a cavernous 12-foot-wide, 20-foot-high, 68-foot-deep hall into the mountain. But, with his dream far from realized, funds dwindling, and clouds of war forming in Europe, the sculptor was forced to cease work on the vault in July 1939.

Despite recurring calls to complete the Hall of Records, a half-century later it remained much the same as it did when crews silenced their drills, wiped the granite dust from their faces, and slowly walked away from one of Borglum's most treasured dreams.

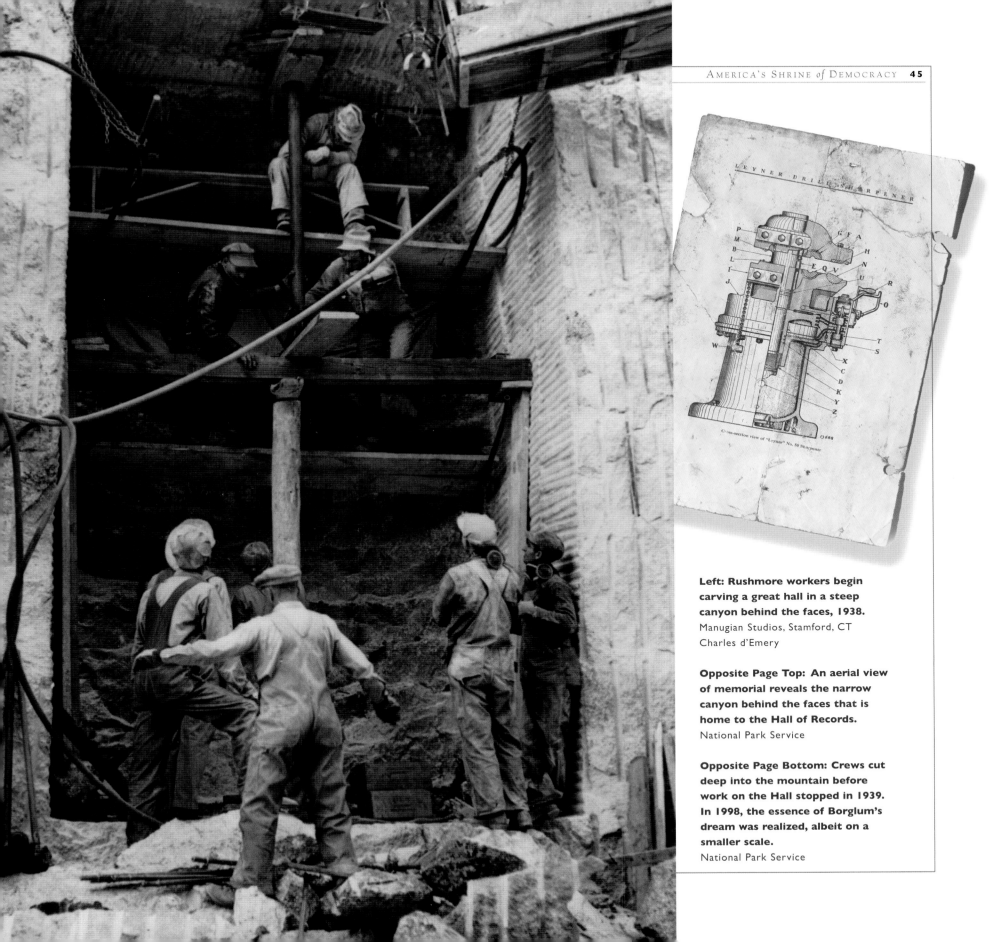

LEYNER DRILL SHARPENER

Cross-section view of "Leyner" No. 59 Sharpener

Left: Rushmore workers begin carving a great hall in a steep canyon behind the faces, 1938.
Manugian Studios, Stamford, CT
Charles d'Emery

Opposite Page Top: An aerial view of memorial reveals the narrow canyon behind the faces that is home to the Hall of Records.
National Park Service

Opposite Page Bottom: Crews cut deep into the mountain before work on the Hall stopped in 1939. In 1998, the essence of Borglum's dream was realized, albeit on a smaller scale.
National Park Service

Above: Lincoln Borglum's drawings showed his father's vision of the Hall, which included mosaic walls of blue and gold lapis, a door of bronze and glass, and busts of great Americans. Aluminum scrolls on which the history of Western civilization would be engraved were to be placed in "damp-proof" tubes and stored in recesses of the Hall, to be opened in 10,000 years.
Lincoln Borglum Collection

Right: Crews constructed a primitive rail line to carry rock from the Hall of Records.
Manugian Studios, Stamford, CT
Charles d'Emery

Opposite Page Right: Borglum's plan also included an entablature in which the history of America would be carved into the mountain.
National Park Service

Left: Gutzon Borglum's daughter, Mary Ellis Borglum Vhay, middle, poses with National Park Service staff during the dedication of the Hall of Records in 1998.
National Park Service

Then in 1998, spurred by a nationwide campaign to preserve and improve the mountain memorial, the National Park Service, the Mount Rushmore National Memorial Society, and the Borglum family united to complete the sculptor's visionary project and preserve Mount Rushmore's story for future civilizations.

On June 22, 1998, the first drilling in 57 years began at Mount Rushmore. Albeit on a much smaller scale than Borglum envisioned, but using the same drilling techniques Rushmore's crews had used to carve the mountain, workers chiseled a small chamber into the Hall's floor, measuring 4 feet deep, 26 inches long, and 16 inches wide.

Then on August 9, 1998, four generations of the Borglum family joined the National Park Service as a teakwood box was gently lowered into a titanium vault set within the chamber. Within the box were 16 porcelain enamel panels etched with the text of the U.S. Constitution and the Declaration of Independence, biographies of each of the presidents depicted, and essays detailing how and why the memorial was carved.

Once sealed, a 1,200-pound capstone of glistening black granite was secured over the vault where it likely will remain for thousands of years — a testament to one man's dream.

"Into this great hall, beautiful

as a temple, we will place

records, the new records,

the purely American

records, of released souls,

of great inventors..."

Gutzon Borglum

RUSHMORE WORKERS WERE A BREED APART

For many of Mount Rushmore's workers, it was just a job, a way to make ends meet during the lean years of the Great Depression.

At the time, these mountain molders didn't know they would take an isolated outcropping in the middle of the continent and blast, drill, and chisel it into a national treasure.

Gutzon Borglum was fond of his crews, and for the most part, they were fond of him. The sculptor was proud that he had taken a roughly hewn bunch of beer-drinking, bar-brawling, out-of-work miners and, like a piece of clay, had shaped them into a crew dedicated to completing an enormous task.

"They knew what they wanted, and they weren't bashful about telling you," recalls driller Norman "Happy" Anderson. "It was just the best job around."

Anderson, who made top wages of $1.25 per hour as an assistant carver was the only worker seriously injured during the 14 years of carving.

Anderson and four others in the crew were joking on June 2, 1940, when they boarded the tramway cage for the regular lift to the top. But all smiles ceased 200 feet from the summit when a small screw let loose, and the wooden tramway began a runaway ride down the mountain.

Although quick action by foreman Matt Reilly and mechanic Howdy Peterson slowed the tram and helped prevent any fatalities, several workers suffered bruises and lacerations when the tram slammed into the platform and sent the crew flying. No one could find Anderson.

Above: Despite placement in precarious positions and the constant use of dynamite and heavy equipment, no workers were killed during construction.
Publisher's Photo Service

Opposite Page: As work on America's Shrine of Democracy nears completion in the summer of 1941, workers take time to pose in front of their colossal creation.
Verne's Photo Shop

"I remember the last thing on my mind was that I would jump and hit the roof of the compressor house," Anderson recalled. "I broke my left arm, all the ribs on my left side, my collar bone, and my insides were busted open so I couldn't eat. Of course I didn't know anything about that for nine days 'til I came to."

Despite the constant danger of working on a mile-high mountain top with explosives and heavy equipment, Mount Rushmore's workers became men with a mission borne out of loyalty to a sculptor and pride in their work. Late in their lives, Rushmore workers still recall the character they helped cut into the giant faces.

"I put the curl in Lincoln's beard, the part in Teddy's hair, and the twinkle in Washington's eye," says Anderson. "It still gives me a thrill to look at it."

Even when lack of funds or severe weather meant enduring layoffs lasting more than a year, many Rushmore workers returned to the mountain time and again hoping to see the project through to its completion.

In March 1983, three years before his death, Lincoln Borglum said it took a special breed of man to climb into a sling seat, be lowered over the edge of a granite cliff, and then wield a drill half his weight.

Left: The workers on Mount Rushmore played just as hard as they worked. One of their pastimes was baseball. Both Gutzon and Lincoln had a love for the sport and at one time only hired workers who could play baseball! In 1939, the Rushmore Team reached the final four at the state tournament in Aberdeen before being eliminated.
Becker's Camera Shop

Opposite Page Top: Lincoln Borglum inspects progress on the Roosevelt head while standing on Jefferson, 1939.
Bell Photo

Opposite Page Below: Alfred Berg, left, and Clyde "Spot" Denton prepare dynamite charges for the afternoon blast.
Bell Photo

"It was just another job at the time but looking back at it, it was quite a feat," says James LaRue, who worked on the memorial for nine years.

Approximately 400 men and women worked at the mountain during six and a half years of actual construction. Of those, less than a dozen were alive in 2003.

But, even though a half-century has dulled some of the memories on the mountain, Rushmore's survivors have come to realize that they created a symbol of freedom recognized around the globe.

"Every time you go up there you are amazed about it," Ed Hayes, long-time hoist house operator at Rushmore, said a few years before his death. "It is one of the greatest works of sculpture of all time. It is one of the wonders of the world."

Hayes recalled the morning Gutzon Borglum walked onto the platform near the hoist house to await a tram ride to the top of the mountain. "He said, 'Hayes, do you see them faces?'" The portly gentleman clad in overalls responded in the negative. "He said, 'They're in there. All I have to do is bring 'em out from under all that rock.'"

Brunner & Lay

STONE and CONCRETE WORKING TOOLS

Catalog No. 31

CHICAGO

NATIONAL PARK SERVICE ROLE

The National Park Service and Mount Rushmore

National Memorial Society began their relationship in 1933 when the memorial was placed under the jurisdiction of the service.

Sculptor Gutzon Borglum and the Mount Rushmore National Memorial Commission remained responsible for the completion of the sculpture. With Borglum's death in 1941 and the decision by the commission and Borglum's son, Lincoln, that the work was essentially finished, the total administrative and protective responsibility was assigned to the National Park Service.

Since that time, Mount Rushmore has been managed under the spirit and intent of the original act that established the National Park Service. This act states that the service ". . . is to conserve the scenery and the natural and historic objects and the wildlife therein and to provide for the enjoyment of the same in such manner and by such means as will leave them unimpaired for the enjoyment of future generations."

Visitor interest has grown dramatically since Borglum first set hammer to chisel, making it necessary for the park service to adapt. The sculpture itself, as well as the remaining models, structures, and tools used in its creation, require specialized care for their protection.

In addition to protecting the carving, the National Park Service has had to make accommodations for increased visitation. In 1989, the National Park Service and Mount Rushmore National Memorial Society entered into an agreement to upgrade all the facilities. Between 1991 and 1998, over $56 million was raised for improvements. Today, Mount Rushmore can boast of modern structures that provide enhanced educational opportunities and better accessibility for disabled and elderly visitors.

However, a hidden and possibly more dangerous threat faces the memorial. Since September 11, 2001, the memorial and its visitors have faced the threat of external terrorist activities. The park service takes these threats seriously and has upgraded security to assure the protection of the sculpture and the safety of visitors and employees.

Sculptor Gutzon Borglum felt the memorial should represent America's first 150 years of its birth, growth, preservation, and development through the accomplishments of the four presidents represented on the mountain. The park service remains committed to offering a quality visitor experience while protecting this unique resource that is the combination of natural-forested setting and man-created heroic art.

Above: Park Service personnel flirt with danger each fall while inspecting the faces and filling cracks in an effort to preserve the memorial.
National Park Service

Opposite Page: Since its completion, the National Park Service has maintained, protected, and interpreted Mount Rushmore National Memorial for freedom-loving people around the world.
National Park Service

MOUNT RUSHMORE TODAY

IMPROVEMENTS:
THE NEW FACE OF A MONUMENT

Gutzon Borglum began carving Mount Rushmore when he was 60 years old, at a time in his life when he knew what only the well-seasoned truly can know — that the legacy left by most men is fleeting.

The irascible sculptor spent the remaining 14 years of his life carving America's legacy along with his own, sending a message of freedom and democracy to future generations while assuring his own immortality.

Even though the conception and execution of Mount Rushmore were clearly Borglum's responsibility, it became apparent early on that it was the duty of the park service to interpret the memorial for the visiting public. With assistance from the Mount Rushmore National Memorial Society, the park service has provided facilities, films, interpretive exhibits, and foreign language translations that explain the history of the memorial.

By the 1980s, nearly a half-century after World War II had halted work on the colossal carvings, the park service was faced with steadily increasing visitation and deteriorating facilities that hampered its ability to tell the Mount Rushmore story. With a growing federal deficit and sorely needed improvements at other park service units, federal funding for major improvements at Mount Rushmore was highly unlikely.

Consequently, in 1989 the Society, which is a non-profit organization, embarked on one of the most ambitious private-sector initiatives in the history of America's national parks. The nationwide campaign raised $25 million, spurred $56 million in improvements, developed new techniques to preserve and monitor the carving as well as protect the memorial's historic artifacts, generated unparalleled media attention for Mount Rushmore, and resulted in new opportunities for visitors to America's Shrine of Democracy.

Above: The talus slope below the mammoth mountain carving bears evidence of the labors undertaken in its creation.
©Paul Horsted/dakotaphoto.com

Opposite Page: Mount Rushmore is home to one of America's most impressive July Fourth holiday fireworks displays.
Paul Niemann

Among the other vast improvements at Mount Rushmore are the Lincoln Borglum Museum, Amphitheater, high-quality concession facilities, Avenue of Flags and Grand View Terrace, enhanced interpretive offerings, improved accessibility for the aged and disabled, expanded parking facilities, and a popular Presidential Trail that leads to the base of the carving.

The Lincoln Borglum Museum opened in 1998 with 5,200 square feet of exhibits, featuring more than 400 photographs and 300 artifacts, a Mount Rushmore History Association bookstore, and two 125-seat theaters. An 80-foot-long photomural taken in 1938 serves as the backdrop for displays of tools used in the carving, while actual film footage shows the tools in use. Interactive exhibits allow visitors to retrieve information about the sculptor and hear interviews with workers on a variety of topics.

The Amphitheater, completed in 1997, is located at the base of Mount Rushmore and hosts one of the most popular interpretive programs in the park service system. The Amphitheater seats 2,500 visitors, is fully accessible, and features a wide range of audiovisual capabilities to stage a variety of events, including one of America's most impressive Independence Day fireworks displays. Each summer

Above: The Sculptor's Studio houses Borglum's original working models and is the site of popular interpretive programs.
South Dakota Tourism

Left: Interpretive exhibits housed in the Lincoln Borglum Museum explore the rationale used in the selection of the four presidents found at Mount Rushmore.
South Dakota Tourism

Opposite Page: The popular Avenue of Flags provides a colorful framework for the four faces of freedom at Mount Rushmore.
Jay Ketel

evening the park service presents a popular program that includes a talk by a ranger and a patriotic film, followed by the lighting of the sculpture with the *National Anthem.*

Spacious concession facilities allow visitors to dine with the presidents and take home a memento of their visit to Mount Rushmore. To accommodate increased visitor length-of-stay caused by expanded interpretive opportunities, a 1,150-space parking structure was completed by the Society in 1998.

Originally established to commemorate America's Bicentennial in 1976, the Avenue of Flags continues to provide a colorful frame to the four faces of freedom on Mount Rushmore. Fifty state flags and six district, territory and commonwealth flags are represented along the walkway to the Grand View Terrace, the main viewing area for the memorial since 1998. Stairways and elevators on either side of the terrace lead to the museum and the Amphitheater.

The Presidential Trail, completed in 1998, affords visitors opportunities to view the memorial up close and to understand the flora and fauna of the Black Hills.

Above: The memorial's Presidential Trail, opened in 1998, affords visitors impressive views of the sculpture, as well as the surrounding forest.
South Dakota Tourism

Right: Mount Rushmore's Amphitheater plays host to films, concerts, ranger talks, and the dramatic night lighting of the memorial.
South Dakota Tourism

Extending in a half-mile loop from the Grand View Terrace to the Sculptor's Studio, the trail passes directly in front of the carving at the base of the rubble pile, providing a unique opportunity to gauge the true scale of the sculpture. Terraces along the trail allow prime viewing of the faces and the surrounding Black Hills. Wayside exhibits explore the reasons Borglum selected each of the presidents for inclusion on Mount Rushmore.

Today's Mount Rushmore would make Gutzon Borglum proud. Through enhanced facilities, exhibits and interpretive programs, visitors gain a greater understanding of the role played by each of the presidents in the birth, growth, preservation and development of the nation, techniques used to create the memorial, the role of the sculptor and his crew, and the flora and fauna of the Black Hills. Through the new Lakota, Nakota and Dakota Heritage Village off the Presidential Trail, visitors encounter the distinct American Indian culture that exists in this region. With several furnished tipis and cultural demonstrators, this area shares the culture of several South Dakota tribes. Near the Grand View Terrace, children of all ages visit the Kids Exploration Area to explore the natural, cultural, and historical aspects of Mount Rushmore and the Black Hills with hands-on activities. Periodically throughout the year, the park also features representatives of other cultures indicative to the Black Hills.

The Mount Rushmore History Association, created by the Society in 1993 to support the park service, operates three bookstores in the park and offers an

Above: The Lakota, Nakota and Dakota Heritage Village educates visitors about American Indian culture.
©Rodger Slott

award-winning audio tour, available in English, German, Spanish, and Lakota. Proceeds from the sale of the association's educational and interpretive publications, as well as its audio tour, support interpretive programs within the park.

The Mount Rushmore Preservation Fund, which was the catalyst behind improvements at Mount Rushmore, continues to provide an ideal example of what public-private sector partnerships can accomplish through creativity, coordination, and cooperation. Together, the National Park Service and the Mount Rushmore National Memorial Society have motivated federal, state, and municipal governments, as well as corporations, foundations, patriotic individuals, and even school children, to preserve and improve one of America's most enduring icons.

Left: Funded through the Mount Rushmore History Association, the Mount Rushmore Audio Tour is a recorded guide at the memorial incorporating narration, music, interviews, sound effects and historic recordings of Gutzon Borglum, Lincoln Borglum, American Indians, and workers. Using a lightweight handheld wand, a visitor can listen to the self-guided tour.

Above left: Mount Rushmore symbolizes in stone the birth, growth, preservation, and development of the United States of America.
©Paul Horsted/dakotaphoto.com

BIBLIOGRAPHY

Borglum, Lincoln. *My Father's Mountain.* Rapid City: Fenwinn, 1965.

Casey, Robert J. and Mary Borglum. *Give the Man Room.* New York: Bobbs-Merrill, 1952.

Cohen, Stan. *Borglum's Mountain.* Missoula: Pictorial Histories, 1983.

Connolly, Joseph P. "The Geology of Mount Rushmore and Vicinity." *The Black Hills Engineer.* Nov. 1930.

Dean, Robert J. *Living Granite.* New York: Viking, 1949.

Fite, Gilbert C. *Mount Rushmore.* Keystone: Mount Rushmore History Association, 2003.

Gordon, Lois and Alan Gordon. *American Chronicle, Six Decades in American Life.* New York: Macmillan, 1987.

Higbee, Paul. *Mount Rushmore's Hall of Records.* Keystone: Mount Rushmore History Association, 1999.

Mount Rushmore National Memorial Commission. Mount Rushmore National Memorial. Interpretive brochures and pamphlets. Washington, D.C.: United States Department of Interior, National Park Service, 1941.

Mount Rushmore National Memorial. Archival material. Keystone: National Park Service, 1925-1990.

Mount Rushmore National Memorial Society. Interpretive brochures and files. Rapid City: N.p, 1930-1990.

Rapid City Journal. Newspaper articles. Rapid City, 1925-1989.

Robinson, Doane. "Inception and Development of the Rushmore Idea." *The Black Hills Engineer.* Nov. 1930.

Runte, Alfred. *National Parks, The American Experience.* Lincoln: University of Nebraska, 1987.

St. George, Judith. *The Mount Rushmore Story.* New York: G.P. Putnam's Sons, 1985.

Shaff, Howard and Audrey Karl. *Six Wars at a Time, The Life and Times of Gutzon Borglum.* Sioux Falls: Augustana College and Permelia, 1985.

Smith, Rex Alan. *The Carving of Mount Rushmore.* New York: Abbeville, 1985.

United States Department of the Interior. Archival material. Washington D.C.: National Park Service. Nd.

William Williamson. *An Autobiography.* Rapid City: N.p, 1964.

Zeitner, June Culp and Lincoln Borglum. *Borglum's Unfinished Dream, Mount Rushmore.* Aberdeen: North Plains, 1976.

ACKNOWLEDGMENTS

The author expresses his deepest appreciation to the following individuals and institutions for assistance, patience, and perseverance while this project was being completed and revised:

The Mount Rushmore Society, including Executive Director Diana Saathoff, Past Presidents Carolyn J. Mollers and the late Ray Aldrich; The Mount Rushmore History Association and Debbie Ketel; The National Park Service and Gerard Baker, Navnit Singh, Dan Wenk, James Popovich and Fred Banks; the Gutzon Borglum family, including the late Mary Ellis Borglum Vhay, James Borglum, and Robin Borglum Carter; photographer and friend Paul Horsted; The Rapid City Journal; Bonnie Krueger; Bill and Alice Groethe; historian, author and friend Rex Alan Smith; the late author Robb DeWall; and; my loving wife, Nyla Griffith.

Archival Photography throughout book:
Johnny Sundby

Below right: Postcard donated by Mr. & Mrs. Jerrel and Patricia Busey

Gutzon Borglum inspecting work on face of Washington Rushmore Memorial
R.I.S.E. Photo